THE LANDSCAPE BOOK OF BRIGHTON PRINTS

Front and back cover:
General View from the Pavilion of Repton's design
for the Pavilion garden—1808

Inside front and back covers and their facing pages:
Four views of The Steine at Brighthelmstone—1788 by Eleanor Lay
Inside front cover:
West side of The Steine—the Manor House and Marlborough House
Facing page:
North side of the Steine with the Royal Pavilion
Inside back cover:
South side of the Steine with Russell House
Facing page:
East side of the Steine

Opposite page:
The Marine Pavilion and Steine—1790 by Thomas Rowlandson

Brighton Books Publishing

Contents

The Carriage Road from Castle Square to St James's and other Important Improvements in the Old Steine.

On the left hand side of the print are some of the first suburban lodging houses. These were built from about 1780 and cut off the views of the sea and downs from the Steine. They were built using fashionable designs from builders' manuals and experience, architects were not involved until some houses were re-fronted in the 1820s. Some are still there today.

Introduction

Henry Smith writes: It may surprise the reader to learn that over a thousand prints of Brighton are recorded.

It gives me particular pleasure to write the introduction to *The Landscape Book of Brighton Prints* as I have known John Coleman, the owner of this outstanding collection of prints, for many years.

It may surprise the reader to learn that over a thousand prints of Brighton are recorded, including five examples by both John Constable and J M W Turner. Before the advent of photography print making was the only method of producing multiple copies, and the topographical view was particularly popular. The print was usually produced from a flat surface of stone, copperplate or block. The artist often cooperated with the engraver to produce the finished work. Colour was added, either by hand or overprinting.

The first important print of Brighton was issued in 1766, a large format one entitled *Lambert's Correct View of Brighthelmstone*. It showed the west side of the Steine and included the site which was later to become the Royal Pavilion. Of all the fine prints in the Coleman collection I would single out the set of engravings of the Steine by Eleanor Lay from 1788. The four are a *tour de force*. Issued in colour they record all the fine buildings of that date. We can see Russell House, Henry Holland's classical Marine Pavilion, the Brighton Manor House and the Robert Adam-designed Marlborough House. The superb reproductions and individual commentaries make this book particularly enjoyable. This fine volume will be highly appreciated by many people, and rightly so.

The West or Garden Front of the Pavilion at Brighton
Marine Palace of his Majesty George IVth.

Foreword

John Coleman writes: I have long wanted my collection of prints to be seen by a wider audience.

My family has been associated with Brighton since the late 18th century. My father, Lewis Cohen, was Mayor of Brighton in 1957, a town councillor for over 30 years, an Alderman, and a Parliamentary candidate for Brighton Kemp Town from 1931 to 1959. His office at 23 New Road is a fine example of Regency architecture, and learning about its history spurred me on to learn more about Brighton's history.

Dudley Rignell was one of the first to show me something of the beauty of the early aquatints of the town, and my interest was fostered by discussions with Henry Smith and Gina Daniels of the Witchball Print and Map shop in The Lanes.

For many years I have had a fascination with prints of Brighton, which are of interest not just for the historical story they tell. They also represent a chapter in the history of art. These prints show how artists such as John Bruce and Thomas Rowlandson were able to make use of techniques such as the aquatint, engraving on copper and steel-plate engraving. The early copper-engraved prints were hand-coloured, giving a particular warmth and vibrancy to them.

I am delighted that the partners in Brighton Books Publishing, Selma Montford and Jacqueline Pollard, have had the foresight and determination to bring this book to print. Selma Montford also deserves the gratitude of the wider community who have an interest in Brighton.

For many years I have had a fascination with Brighton prints and have long wanted my collection to be seen by a wider audience. This book will make that possible.

The Riding School in the Dome
Designed by William Porden in 1803.
Aquatint by M Dubourg 1824.

The Riding School in the Dome was designed to incorporate some of the characteristics of Indian architecture as perceived at the time. It was based on the Corn Market in Paris, with stables for the horses on the ground floor and quarters for the stable hands round the upper floor balcony.

The Pavilion View of the Stable Front

Mike Jones writes: The original accounts held at Kew document the garden's creation and list the plants used.

The Pavilion garden has developed over the two hundred years from 1783—the year the Prince of Wales first visited Brighton. His first rented house had a tiny circular lawn fronting the Steine and Great East Street running along the rear western side. The garden was soon enlarged as a consequence of the Prince offering to drain the Steine in return for extra land. The garden boundary was protected by a railed ha-ha, allowing uninterrupted views from the windows but preventing people and livestock from entering.

By 1801 the garden had been further enlarged, to designs by Henry Holland and planting by Samuel Lapidge, who had been an assistant to Capability Brown. The next phase of the garden, in 1803, involved closing Great East Street on the understanding that the Prince would build New Road, which still forms the western boundary today. For this extension Humphry Repton produced designs for a Moghul garden, but they were not used. Among his ideas was a square pool as a centrepiece for the Western lawns, illustrated opposite.

The eventual garden and final Pavilion was designed by John Nash from 1813. That garden was planted by William Townsend Aiton, the Royal Gardener at Kew, and John Furner, whose family had owned the market gardens which were purchased by the Prince to build New Road. Furner was then employed as gardener at the Pavilion. The original accounts held at Kew document the garden's creation and list the plants used. The garden has been listed by English Heritage.

Repton's Design for the Pavilion View of the Stable Front 1808

Hand coloured aquatint.

The Royal Marine Library

Christopher Hawtree writes: Who, on looking at this picture, cannot help but delight in the eighteenth-century rise of the congenial library?

John Wells wrote of the London Library:, "There is, as in most libraries, a heavily charged erotic atmosphere in the Reading Room, a girl undoing a button of her cardigan lifts a head from every armchair." One of Barbara Pym's 1930s diaries records her mind straying similarly as she surveys other readers during her visits to the Bodleian's Reading Rooms.

And so, as one looks across this summer's evening scene at the Royal Marine Library, it is not entirely fanciful to surmise that the minds of the gentlemen, and of the plentiful ladies, are not completely focussed on the performances given by the pair above them. Who knows what they are thinking? Some might be wishing that they could reach the books behind the two speakers.

We are now so accustomed to public libraries that one can forget that these only came into being with the 1850 Public Libraries Act. Prior to that libraries had been privately accumulated or run by subscription. Many people, fearful of the masses, wanted to keep it that way. As the free libraries today charge ever more heavily for services whilst their own stocks dwindle, are we returning to a country in which the private library—one's own or such places as the Royal Marine Library—is in the ascendant? That would be lamentable.

On looking at this picture who cannot help but delight in the 18th century rise of the congenial library and revel in all that it contains, its abundant sense of life's possibilities in all their forms?

2, 3, 5 and 8, or a Summer's Evening at the Royal Marine Library, Brighton
C W Wing ca1830.

2, 3, 5 and 8 was the title of a musical entertainment, a concert performance which is being given in the library. Music was part of library life at the time.

The Race Ground

Derek Burns writes: The gallows that can be seen in the middle distance is for the weighing in of jockeys, not the hanging of losing riders.

The print shows the races in their very early days. Brighton probably had races in the 18th century, as a Race Post is noted on the Steine in 1713, but the first known race was in August 1770 between Dr Kipping, the local surgeon, and Mr Shergold of The Castle inn. It was a four-mile gallop over the Downs for a ten guineas prize.

Another 13 years passed before the first proper races, as listed in the *Racing Calendar*, were held. A year later, in 1784, the Prince of Wales attended; the year after that stalls for local publicans to sell beer were allowed, and the year after that a Race Ball was held. The Races had become an institution.

On those early Race Days the betting started in the morning down on the Steine, and everyone waited until the first bets were laid by Lord Egremont or Sir Charles Bunbury. The races themselves were run in heats gradually eliminating the slowest horses, each 'race' consisting of up to eight heats if there were numerous entries. Sometimes race meetings went on until 8 pm or until night fell. For four-mile races the horses started at the grandstands, went out to the two mile post, round a loop and all the way back to the stands. Poor horses after several heats of that!

The gallows that can be seen in the middle distance is for the weighing in of jockeys, not the hanging of losing riders. The grandstand shown was burnt down in 1796 when the family that was occupying it between race meetings were careless. The blaze was seen for 30 miles and caused great alarm as many thought it signalled Bonaparte's invasion.

Race Ground
by Thomas Rowlandson, etched and aquatinted for The Excursion to Brighthelmstone *by Samuel Alken 1790 ."A handsome and convenient Stand sufficiently capacious to receive a great Number of Spectators, is erected on the Course".*

Bathing Machines

Geoffrey Mead writes: the distinction between lowly paid locals performing services and moneyed visiting 'swells' . . . is one that persists

The two halves of Brighton's economy are shown here. Down on the beach are a group of fishermen, whose trade had precariously sustained the town for the first five hundred or so years of its life. Scrambling down the cliff staircase come the first of the visitors who were to sustain it for the next two hundred years.

Erosion of the foreshore and adjacent cliff—dramatically portrayed here—had caused the town to fall on hard times, and in the 1720s Daniel Defoe records it as being in danger of being "devoured by the water" and about to be abandoned. This terminal decline was turned around in the mid 18th century through Dr Russell's promotion of the sea as a health-giving medium, a place where copious draughts of ozone could be inhaled, where clients could be 'dipped', and—bizarrely—where health giving seawater potions could be imbibed.

This print catches the cusp of this turn-around. The first beginnings of a resort infrastructure are there in the stairway, the rickety safety fence on the cliff top and the provision of a number of bathing machines with their attendants, meeting a need for a service that was previously not known. Unseen, but obviously nearby in the town, would be the lodgings, assembly rooms, bath houses and taverns associated with the seaside. It all led eventually to the city by the sea. But the distinction between lowly-paid locals performing services and moneyed visiting 'swells' implied in the print is one that persists to the present day.

Bathing Machines
drawn by Thomas Rowlandson,
aquatint by Samuel Alken 1790.
Excursion to Brighthelmstone
by Wigstead and Rowlandson.

The Chain Pier Brighton

Gavin Henderson writes: The piers became . . . a fantastical republic of fun, a place for meeting, mating and make believe.

From the middle of the 19th century a rash of piers began to sprout from the British coastline, but there had been tentative structures earlier in the century such as the suspension, or chain, piers at Leith (near Edinburgh) and at Brighton in the 1820s. These were built essentially for the needs of marine transport, and that is what is illustrated here. The Chain Pier was initially built to stop the milking of the cross-channel passenger trade, where being ferried ashore cost more than the passage across the Channel. But to their surprise the owners of these early landing stages found that they could also make money from visitors strolling on them.

It was this discovery that created the new wave of pier building, driven by the wider brief for pleasure and fashion. The pier became the place to be seen; windbreaks and kiosks meant people could sit and take refreshments; bandstands provided entertainment to the elegant Society parading in their new frocks. It wasn't long before the pier heads were crowned with fine pavilions, often in the Moorish style, with onion domes and minarets reflecting the influence of Brighton's Royal Pavilion.

The piers became a classless place of departure, a near biblical experience of walking safely above the waves, leaving behind the cares of everyday life on the mainland, joining the throng in a world governed by a naval hierarchy of uniformed pier masters and deckhands, a fantastical republic of fun, a place for meeting, mating and make-believe. And all this started with the Chain Pier in 1820.

The Chain Pier Brighton
by George Bryant Campion.
Aquatint by Charles Hunt 1838.

The Chain Pier builder, Captain Samuel Brown, used his previous experience of building harbour jetties and a suspension bridge in Scotland to create a unique pier with suspension chains and towers. The towers were constructed in cast iron. The suspension chains were securely fixed to the cliff and then laid over each tower and fixed to the seabed at the landing stage end. The deck, made of iron and timber, was then hung from vertical rods fixed at intervals along the chains.

The Chain Pier during the Tempest of 1824

Fred Gray writes about: Piering into the Future . . . presenting alternative architectural and engineering possibilities . . .

This print shows the full fury of the sea attacking Brighton's first Pier. It did not long survive these batterings. Neither did many other piers erected around our coast. The 40-odd surviving piers are fewer than half the number that existed a century ago. What future is there for piers—in essence an architecture and entertainment created for the 19th century seaside? In one view piers should be "allowed to slip beneath the waves" as tired, redundant structures, symbolic of an outmoded English seaside.

Brighton's West Pier, despite being a Grade I listed structure and eulogised for its iconic beauty, seemingly confirms such a view. Closed in 1975, three decades later there it is a ruined skeleton, destroyed by storm, arson attacks, bureaucratic dithering and private sector self-interest, in spite of passionate attempts to save it. And yet a short distance from the ruin, the Palace Pier (now unhappily known as Brighton Pier) sparkles with lights and heaves with visitors and swirling funfair rides. This commercially successful pier reveals there is nothing pre-ordained about the fate of seaside architecture.

Elsewhere in Europe, particularly on the Baltic coast of the unified Germany, new piers—some remodelled on lost structures—have become a tool of seaside regeneration. Woefully, in Britain, too often piers are seen as part of the problem and not part of the solution. The situation may change, and in the first years of the new century there are interesting proposals for new piers in Brighton and other seaside towns, presenting alternative architectural and engineering possibilities focussed on the future rather than the past.

The Chain Pier During the Late Tempest of 1824

Plan of Kemptown Brighton

Chris Horlock writes: The final result, even only partly built, seems a spectacular success story.

Thomas Read Kemp, a wealthy landowner, speculator and one-time MP for Arundel, began his bold venture of creating a new, self-sufficient town for the rich nobility on the eastern outskirts of Brighton in 1823. This print shows the original vision, at least twice the size as it stands today. Kemp employed architects Amon Wilds and Charles Augustin Busby for the general plan and to design the house frontages.

Lewes Crescent, Sussex Square to the north and the extensive terraces either side, were completed by 1828; Chichester Terrace was added later. Various developers completed the insides of the houses so the interior layouts varied considerably. Many were not fully finished for twenty or thirty years, simply frontages standing held up by scaffolding. Parts of the plan as drawn, the large squares at the rear and the rows of mews, were never built.

Part of the attraction of the estate was that the houses appeared to be part of a classical palace. The dimensions remain unrivalled; the span of Lewes Crescent is nearly 850 feet—some 200 feet wider than the Royal Crescent at Bath. The final result, even only partly built, seems a spectacular success story. Architecturally it undoubtedly was, but financially it proved a complete disaster. It ended with spending going through the roof, forcing Kemp to flee Britain in 1837 to escape creditors. In January 1844 a statement that Kemp was an outlaw was fixed to the door of St Peter's Church and he died in Paris just four months later.

Kemptown Brighton
Erecting on the East Cliff
on the Estate of T R Kemp Esq MP.
To whom this plate is respectively dedicated
by the Obedt Servt J Bruce
Aquatint by John Bruce from his own sketch ca1826

The complete plan—with with two squares on either side of Sussex Square, and two rows of buildings with housing for servants and stables behind the two sides of Lewes Crescent—was never completed.

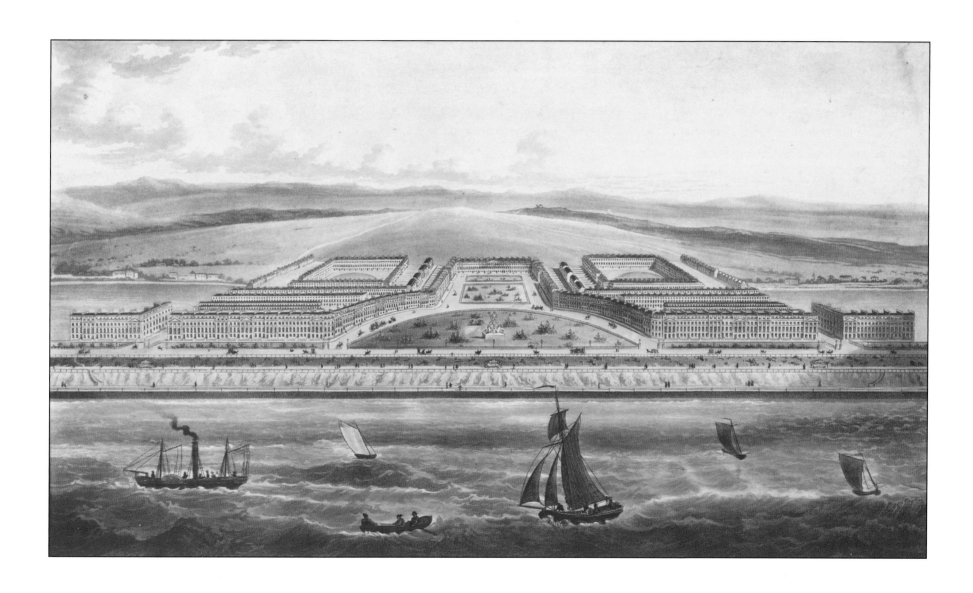

Kemp Town Brighton

Derek Granger writes: the gleaming white stucco facades of Kemp Town present a panorama which dazzles the eye.

On a clear blue day with wispy clouds racing overhead the gleaming white stucco facades of Kemp Town present a panorama which dazzles the eye. Majestic Sussex Square, the imposing Chichester and Arundel terraces, and the billowing curves of Lewes Crescent make this superb architectural assembly seem one of the most handsome places in the world. I have lived here for nearly fifty years and never for a moment tired of it, or the constantly changing marine light. To walk through the Enclosures or to idle quietly there on a Summer's day is to enjoy the pleasures of a charmingly cultivated miniature park, but one which retains just enough untamed rusticity to give corners of it the feeling of a secret domain.

The creation of Kemp Town had a troubled history, but when eventually it was completed the great nabobs of the day took up residences. Four Victorian prime ministers stayed there, the sixth Duke of Devonshire became famous for his prodigal hospitality, Victoria and Albert left their children in the Enclosures with a Lady-in-Waiting whilst they drove to Rottingdean, Edward VII was greeted by a rowdy crowd when he arrived to stay with his daughter, the Princess Royal, and the Marquess of Bristol lent his house in Sussex Square to the exiled King of France, Louis-Philippe. Rich in history, Kemp Town still seems very much alive with it today.

Kemp Town Brighton
by George Bryant Campion 1838
drawn and Engraved by Chas Hunt. Aquatint.

Brunswick Town adjoining Brighton

Michael Ray writes: Between 1810 and 1820 Brighton grew faster than any other town in England

Between 1810 and 1820 Brighton grew faster than any other town in England and by the early 1820s all the available land in the town centre had been developed. Kemp began his famous new town on the eastern frontier whilst to the west the tide of development reached the parish of Hove. There the open land was part of Wick Farm owned by the Reverend Thomas Scutt, a member of a Brighton brewing family. Kemp persuaded him to start a similar new town, to be named Brunswick, and building began in 1824, a year later than Kemptown.

The estate was not developed by Scutt. Instead the bare building plots were sold provided that the buildings were approved by Scutt's overall designer, Charles Augustin Busby. This print by J Bruce shows an idealised picture of Busby's intentions and there are several differences from what was actually achieved. Brunswick Square and Terrace were complete by 1829. The Market building shown to the east was also built, though further north, and after a chequered career now houses a fine performance venue in Upper Market Street, off Western Road. The large building on the east of what became Waterloo Street was never built but St Andrew's Church, designed by Charles Barry, was erected instead. Waterloo Street and Lansdowne Place are rather grander in concept than reality. There is no sign of the two sets of narrow-fronted houses in the Square which replaced roads leading to the Mews.

Despite these omissions Brunswick Town still retains a separate community feel today and its tall, sweeping terraces sustain a very lively, indigenous life.

Brunswick Square and Adjacent Buildings
Adjoining Brighton
Aquatint by John Bruce after Charles Busby 1829.

There are two houses on the skyline of the print, in addition to a couple of the ubiquitous windmills. The square building to the right was The Temple, Thomas Kemp's home that, albeit much-changed, today houses the Brighton & Hove High School. The more modest building in the centre, with the imaginary imposing driveway to it, is Wick House.

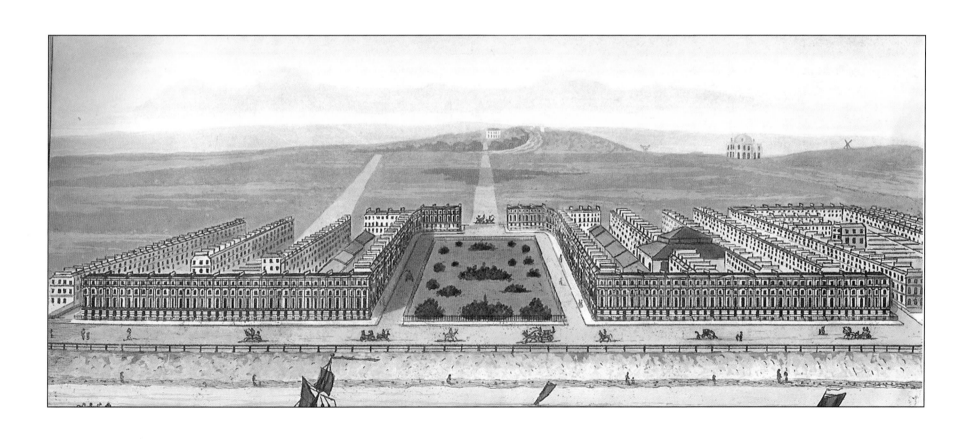

St Peter's Church

Jacqueline Pollard writes: In 2005 the Brighton & Hove Deaneries Pastoral Strategy Group recommended the redundancy of St Peter's . . .

This 1839 print of St Peter's Church is seen from Richmond Place ten years after its completion in 1828. It was built on an area once known as Richmond Green, situated between York Place and Richmond Place, and immediately became a significant landmark in the town. St Peter's was originally built as a Chapel of Ease to the Parish Church of St Nicholas but became Brighton's Parish Church in 1874.

The competition to design it was won by Charles Barry, then a youthful 28, who went on to design, in the same early Gothic Revival style, the Houses of Parliament. The church was built in Portland stone, which has not weathered well. It measured 150 feet by 70 feet and had a nave and five bays with aisles, galleries, a vaulted ceiling and hexagonal apse. The original design had a spire that was never built. Barry's apse was demolished in 1898 and an extension designed by George Somers Clark replaced it—in Sussex sandstone thus creating the two-toned appearance of today. The decoration behind the altar in the chapel is in memory of the Brighton troops who died in the First World War. The stained glass window above the High Altar by Charles Kemp is a memorial to Queen Victoria.

In 2005 the Brighton & Hove Deaneries Pastoral Strategy Group recommended the redundancy of St Peter's as a place of worship, and the redevelopment of the interior for other useful purposes. The Parochial Church Council is now considering ways to work with other denominations and faiths to maintain the spiritual work of the church that has served the community of Brighton for so long.

St Peter's Church Brighton 1839
From the New Church at the entrance of the Town.
Including the Marine Palace of
her Majesty Victoria the First. Drawn Engraved &
Published by Ino Bruce. Aquatint

Bird's Eye View of Brighton

Selma Montford writes: Brighton is a city of contrasts, a palace next to poverty.

Brighton is a city of contrasts, a palace next to poverty. This view from St Peter's Church highlights the juxtaposition of the Royal Pavilion—along with the grand buildings facing the Steine and the wide sweep of the roadway round its central gardens—against the chaotic jumble of small dwellings stretching up Carlton Hill. Brighton was typical of Victorian towns—the wealthy needed their servants to live close by, working people and tradesmen needed to live near the town centre for work, fishermen needed to live near the shore. This has been referred to as "privies and pandemonium", but also as "an essential part of the economy of the city".

"The inhabitants of Carlton Hill were united by poverty, and built up strong support networks within the community to help them survive the rigours of their lives. Not everyone had extended families, but everyone had neighbours. The demolition of such a neighbourhood is not just the destruction of buildings, it is also the destruction of a complex social support system. "*Backyard Brighton: Photographs and Memories of Brighton in the Thirties.*

R J Weedon wrote in the *Evening Argus* in 1988: "The people who lived in these houses were good, clean, working class people. They kept their houses spotless, and the front doorsteps and each bit of pavement was swept and washed nearly every morning. In the summer evenings we would sit out on the front steps enjoying a laugh with our friendly neighbours. Life was hard, but those small, jumbled houses rising up the hill were places of happiness as much as the grand ones on the Steine."

Bird's Eye View of Brighton
From the New Church at the Entrance of the Town.
Including the Marine Palace of
Her Majesty Queen Victoria the First.
John Bruce: aquatint by the artist, 1839.

The Town Hall is shown beyond the Dome.
In the foreground, Richmond Terrace is on the left and
St George's Place is on the right.
All the front gardens have disappeared and
many of the balconies have gone.

North Laine *ca*1850

Geoffrey Mead writes: The prevailing southwest wind, blew the pollution away from the seaside terraces and crescents.

This spectacular view of the town's northern suburbs—one of an industrial community—is pictured from the slopes of Hilly Laine—now Hanover. It presents a very different scene, from the usual image of the resort. The foreground shows the genteel world of grassed enclosures, strolling gentry and smart carriages, backed by tall bow-fronted dwellings, the society church of St Peter's soaring over all. But the area behind contains packed terraced housing for the workers, intermixed with smoking factories, workshops, stabling, cowsheds, slaughter-yards, and the railway terminus, a social mixture noted in many nineteenth century cities.

The smoking chimneys of Evershed's soap works, the Regent iron and brass foundry, Eede Butts & Sons' sawmills, were turning out the goods that Brighton needed as a large urban manufacturing centre. Yet only 20 years earlier the local press could say "Brighton is a town of few manufactures". North Laine, with it's lack of access to the fashionable Steine and promenade, and it's gently sloping hillsides, acted as a manufacturing and warehousing buffer-zone between the rural hinterland and the urban centre; where timber, stone, animals, malt and grain were brought in by train to be processed into furniture and metal components, foodstuffs, bacon and beer. The prevailing southwest wind, as seen here, blew the pollution away from the seaside terraces and crescents.

The third element of this scene is the semi-rural fringe of windmills, open land and detached housing along the Dyke Road ridge, showing the town as having a growing suburban component.

Gloucester Hotel, Railway Terminus and St Peter's Church
G Ruff, copper engraving by W J Alias ca1850.

Hudson's Mill and Dyke Road, then known then as Church Hill, are on the skyline. In the centre Trafalgar Street runs up to the Station under the iron bridge at the top. The area between Church Street and Cheapside already includes the lay-out of the streets in North Laine.

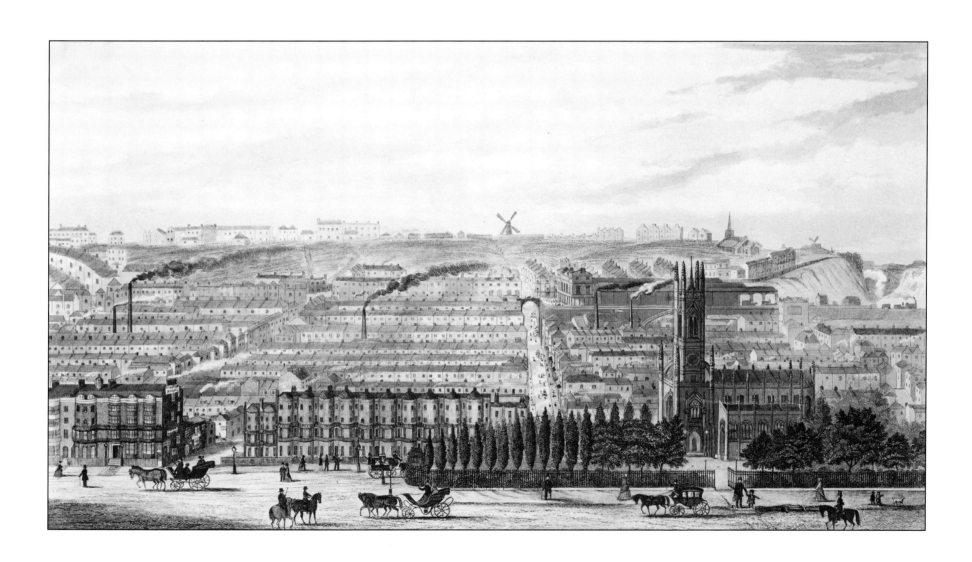

Interior of the New Market Place

Geoffrey Mead writes: . . . many traders operated from the steps of the new Town Hall giving a Covent Garden-like ambience . . .

The importance of a market to Brighton's economy can be judged by the fact that of just seven streets named in the early town, one was designated Market Street. That market was located at Bartholomews, midway between the farmers of North Street and the fishermen on the beach, and likewise equidistant between the grand houses of the town's west end and the crowded tenements of East Street - a classic market location.

By 1830 the population was over 40,000 and the need to feed this vast influx meant a new market was required. The palatial structure pictured here probably owes much to artistic licence but the reality itself lasted until the early 20th century. The 'vittals' on display - game and beef joints, fish and cabbages, herbs and geese - reflect the final stage of a complex food distribution system that developed as Brighton grew. Within a few years the *Gardeners' Magazine* noted the town's suburbs as replete with extensive graperies at Queen's Park and salad-producing glasshouses "cultivated with great spirit" at Rose Hill, above The Level.

Brighton's social elite meant a ready market for such luxury crops; more mundane vegetables such as potatoes were noted by the magazine as coming in from "the fine sandy soils" of Arundel and Storrington. Adjacent to the Market many traders operated from the steps of the new Town Hall giving a Covent Garden-like ambience to civic proceedings. This colourful scene was 'tidied up' in 1937 when the new fruit market was built at the foot of Carlton Hill, paradoxically on an old market garden. The Wholesale Fruit and Vegetable market has now been moved to Hollinbury.

Interior of the New Market Place
John Bruce aquatint by the artist c1830.

The Market, designed and constructed in the form of a T was opened in 1830 , with the stem of the T acting as a Butcher's Row and the cross-piece as the Fish Market. Vegetables seem to have been under the arcades, along with other stalls selling poultry.

The National School, Church Street

Selma Montford writes: they were outstanding, both as individual buildings and as a symphony of shapes . . . materials and detail.

'The junction of New Road with Church Street is the remnant of one of the most magical examples of good townscape in Brighton. It included the Greek Revival Unitarian church and next door a fine example of Regency architecture—once Drury's, the theatrical costumiers, now the office of John Coleman, the collector of these prints. On the corner is the black-painted pebble and bow fronted building, once the Regent Hotel. With the rare Regency Gothic National School in Church Street, the focal point of that end of New Road, they were outstanding, both as individual buildings and as a symphony of shapes, proportions, materials and detail.

Tragically the National School has gone, demolished in 1971 for a road widening which has never, and now never will, take place. It was destroyed during a postal strike which prevented the Grade II listing document being received by the Council. Now the only remaining Regency Gothic buildings in Brighton are the Gothic House in Western Road, now shops with flats above; and the Swan Downer School at the bottom of Dyke Road, currently a night club.

Anthony Dale, founder of the Regency Society of Brighton and Hove, considered the demolition of the National School to be "the most shocking demolition that has taken place in Brighton . . . a criminal folly". Other follies were the demolition of two of four buildings known as the Blues and the Buffs—1 and 2 Old Steine—in 1928, also for road widening; Waterloo Place in Lewes Road; Attree Villa in Queen's Park; Grenville Place—now buried under Churchill Square; and the Bedford Hotel.

The National School, Church Street
This print is respectively dedicated by his obliged servant H Mew, the first builder, to the Revd H M Wagner, Vicar of Brighton. Lithographed and printed by Day and Hague 1831.

Pool Valley During the Storm of 1850

Sue Berry writes: The thunderstorm of Wednesday 17 July 1850 lasted for about an hour . . .

For centuries Pool Valley was called the Pool, the addition of Valley only coming into use in the 19th century. It was open at the sea end and small boats could be beached in it. Until about 1810 hog boats—Brighton fishing vessels— were built there.

Pool Valley was once the outlet for the Wellesbourne, a seasonal chalk stream which surfaced and turned parts of the Steine into a marshy area when the water table rose. It added to the flooding when it overflowed the primitive outfall sewer built by the Prince of Wales in the 1790s.

The deluge of 17 July lasted for about an hour and the town's limited drainage system utterly failed to cope. Pool Valley was but one of the low-lying areas that suffered, but it took the brunt of water pouring down into it from the Steine. The raising of a bank across its southern front in 1818 to support the town's first seafront had created a lethal dam. Even today the seafront road is higher than Pool Valley.

This print shows a considerable number of older buildings in the middleground. Creak's Baths were originally Awsiter's and opened in the 1760s. Most of the other low-lying buildings date from the 18th century. The buildings to the left of the baths are Regency in style, probably of the 1820s and still standing, albeit somewhat altered.

Pool Valley became a transport and cinema centre between the two World Wars and all the small buildings around Creak's were lost, but some nearby are with us still.

Pool Valley During the Storm at Brighton
published by W J Leathern and J Watkins.

On Wednesday evening, 17 July 1850, between 6 and 7 o'clock a most terrible and destructive Thunderstorm, accompanied with a most complete deluge of rain burst over the Town, raging above an hour and occasioning much injury and loss of property, inundating Pool Valley and other parts of the Town to the depth of several feet.

View of Brighton Station

Jacky Marsh-Hobbs writes: . . . triangles of decoration . . . a mixture of designs incorporating thistles, ivy and dolphins.

Brighton Station opened on the 21 September 1841, the same day as the line from London to Brighton. The Shoreham line had been operational from May the previous year. This early picture of David Mocatta's magnificent Italianate station shows its original splendour with a round-arched colonnade. Between the nine arches are triangles of decoration, these being a mixture of designs incorporating thistles, ivy and dolphins. This wonderful façade is now obscured by H E Wallis's addition of the glass and cast-iron *porte cochere* erected in 1882. Still visible, however, on the back of the building on the first floor is an identical row of windows as on the front facade, with alternating triangular and segmental pediments.

As headquarters of The London to Brighton Railway the first floor contained the Board Room and offices, including the Engineering Department for the whole line. On the ground floor the London and the Shoreham passengers were kept very much apart. A door to the left, just under the elevated colonnade, went into the Shoreham booking office, on one side of which were situated the Gentlemen's Waiting Room and lavatories with the equivalent Ladies' rooms behind. The layout was duplicated on the east side for the London passengers.

Passengers were not permitted to smoke a the station or in any of the carriages.

View of the Brighton Station
of the London & Brighton Railway
respectively inscribed and dedicated to
The Directors, Shareholders and Engineers
by David Mocatta ARCHT FSA.
Lithograph drawn on stone by G Childs from the
original drawing by David Mocatta, which was
exhibited at the Royal Academy in 1841.

Endpiece—City of Angles

Simon Montgomery writes: I knew . . . that these pages would be bound to surprise and delight.

Seeing these prints for the first time was a revelation. I felt as if I was walking into a particularly elegant place of worship and catching my breath as I crossed the threshold.

I was in the Brighton Business Centre, an old ecclesiastical building, which proved to be a perfect setting. I laid out each print on the top of an old mahogany chest . The sun was streaming through an arched Victorian window. Every page filled with light. Every page had a new angle and poise. Thoughts and feelings flooded into sharp relief. These were visions and revisions, familiar places seen from unusual vantage points and illustrations and maps that pointed to the buried treasure trove of twittens and the Town Hall. This book, I was sure, could become a masterpiece. Brighton revealed in all its Bohemian Rhapsody. Fishing town to global village in 48 pages. Here it might be, I thought. At last, positioned now and framed forever, the first full visual history to genuinely catch the spirit of 'The Place to Be' in all its idiosyncratic glory.

I knew that morning that these pages would be bound to surprise and delight. In the end piece is my beginning. Here it is in my hands, right here, right now. A single volume, a local source and all that I will ever need to teach and tell me about the city that I love.

Praise you Brighton.

The Town Hall
Brighton grew rapidly in the 1820s prompting the Brighton Commissioners to propose a new town hall and market in Bartholomews. The designs were put out to competition, the winner was Thomas Cooper, designer of the original Bedford Hotel. The Town Hall was opened in 1830.

Sponsors

Brighton Books Publishing gratefully acknowledges contributions from those who have made the publication of this book possible:

Leslie Wilmot, also in memory of Elfrida Oldfield 1922-2005.

Austin Gray, Carr & Priddle, Peter Overill Associates and

Ritelands Co Ltd

The Picture Frame Company Ltd who have funded the launch of *The Landscape Book of Brighton Prints*

Acknowledgements
Our special thanks to John Coleman who has allowed us to create this book with some of the prints from his collection.

Thanks to all who contributed the commentaries; their perceptions provide another dimension to the prints.

This book has been produced by several pairs of hands:

Editor and Designer: Selma Montford

Book Design: Simon Montgomery, Computer Box College

Editorial Consultant: Derek Burns

Proof reading: Edwin Bray

Photographic origination: Yiorgos Nikiteas

Colour corrections: Adrian Montford

Printed by Delta Press, 2 Goldstone Street, Hove BN3 3RJ

Brighton Books Publishing is a partnership of Selma Montford & Jacqueline Pollard

Landscape Book of Brighton Prints. Published 2005. ISBN 1-901454-09-6

A Scene at the Devil's Dyke near Brighton
Devil's Dyke, a prominent viewpoint 712 feet high on the crest of the Downs north of Brighton, became a part of the resort's attractions from the early 19th century

Current List of Titles

Available by post only from the publishers. Please add £2.00 p & p per book or £3.00 for two or more books. Also available from bookshops.

The Vanishing Villas of Preston & Withdean by Selma Montford,
Jacqueline Pollard & Robert Sanderson (1996). ISBN 1-901454-00-2 @ £5.50

Dr Brighton's Indian Patients: December 1914 - January 1916
by Joyce Collins (!997) ISBN 1-901454-01-0@ £5.50

Photographs Memories of Brighton & Hove
by Mark Whenman (1998). ISBN 1-901454-02-9 @ £1.00.

Little to Spare and Nothing to Waste: a Brighton Boyhood in the Hungry Thirties by Robert Haywood (1998) ISBN 1-901454-03-7 @ £5.50.

Memories and Photographs of Brighton in the 20s & 30s
by H T Dawes (2002). ISBN 1-901454-05-3 @ £6.99.

Churchill Square Revisited : a lost Brighton community
by Andrew Walker (2002) ISBN 1-901454-06-1 @ £6.99.

Rose Hill to Roundhill : a Brighton Community'
 (2004) ISBN 1-901454-08-8 @ £9.99

Preston : Downland Village to Brighton Suburb'
(2004) ISBN 1-901454-07-X @ £9.99

Blighty Brighton about Brighton in the First World War
(1991) ISBN 0-904733-55-6 @ £4.95

Past & Present: the Story of Blaker's Park (1994) ISBN 0-9522856-0-6 @ £5.00

Brighton Books Publishing 10 Clermont Road Brighton BN1 6SG
phone 01273-509209 fax 01273-502018 email info@brightonbooks.co.uk
www.brightonbooks.org.uk

Plan of Brighton with the latest Improvements to 1827
drawn to accompany Bruce's Guide to Brighton,
published in 1825 and updated in 1828.

This map shows the extent of the resort which only 40 years previously had been contained within the confines of the Old Town. Brighton's role as the premier resort is shown here with the fashionable Chain Pier and the new coastal highway, King's Road; Brighton (now Queen's) Park and the racecourse on the eastern fringe, and to the north the new St Peter's Church and Ireland's Pleasure Grounds. Major upmarket housing projects, to east and west, stand out clearly, as does the difference between the streets developed on the rigid field strips to the north and east in contrast to the haphazard pattern in the Old Town.

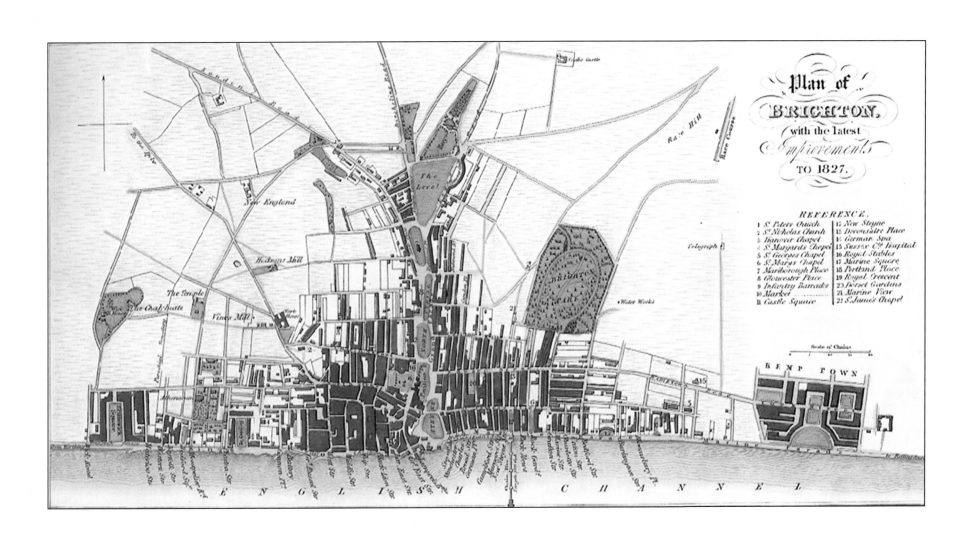